HOW I ALMOST DESTROYED MY RELATIONSHIP:

Keys to Effective Communication in Relationships

Linda T. Barbara

TABLE OF CONTENT

CHAPTER 1 : Starting Afresh

I'm certain you've heard this saying previously "communication is the key to any relationship." It sounds cliche yet it's valid. I believe it's truly simple to let individuals know that communication is significant in a sound relationship yet it's not as simple to clear up how to convey. What's more, if we're never shown how to utilize this key, we'll always be unable to make the way for solid communication.

Communication is characterized as a ton of things yet my number one definition incorporates, "the effective conveying or sharing of thoughts and sentiments". I generally say I'm an extraordinary talker, yet I need to likewise be a similarly extraordinary audience to be an incredible communicator. Communication is tied in with putting yourself out there in a solid manner, paying attention to your accomplice when they are doing likewise, and sincerely hearing and engrossing what the other individual needs to say. It is never beyond any good time to begin once more by first including; positive self-talk, Being credible, and making enhancements for your fearlessness,

Positive Self-Talk:

Self-talk is your inward exchange. It's affected by your psyche brain, and it uncovers your considerations, convictions, questions, and thoughts. Self-talk can be both negative and positive. It very well may be empowering, and it tends to trouble. A lot of your self-talk relies upon your character. Assuming that you're a confident person, your self-talk might be more confident and positive. The inverse is for the most part evident on the off chance that you will generally be a cynic.

Here are a few instances of how individuals can bring an end to the propensity for negative self-talk. Good self-talk helps an individual have a positive outlook on themselves. It can energize and propel an individual to continue onward, look on the "splendid side," and put things into point of view. Instances of positive self-talk are, "I'm truly glad for myself," "I'm getting along admirably," or "That isn't perfect, yet it very well may be more regrettable". Step-by-step instructions to make self-talk more certain and more positive. Seeing pessimistic self-talk and turning it around before it grabs hold can assist with people thinking all the more emphatically and change their ways of behaving. It is proposed that positive or pessimistic self-talk turns into a propensity that individuals can change. Good self-talk is an inner discourse that helps an individual have a positive outlook on themselves. An individual can utilize good self-converses with thinking hopefully and feel spurred.

Recognizing negative self-talk is the most vital move toward thinking all the more emphatically. An individual's correspondence with themselves is called self-talk or inner discourse. It is a characteristic mental cycle. Individuals could take part in self-talk more when they face deterrents or difficulties. Individuals utilize self-talk either quietly or address themselves without holding back.

The most important phase in making self-talk more sure is to distinguish negative reasoning. An individual can see how they talk

with themselves when confronted with difficulties. It might assist with recording instances of negative self-talk. These situations are instances of when and how you can transform negative self-talk into positive self-talk. Once more, it takes practice. Perceiving your very own portion of negative self-talk in these situations might assist you with creating abilities to flip the idea when it happens.
Negative: That is excessively troublesome.
Positive: It sounds testing.
Negative: I can't make it happen.
Positive: I will do my absolute best.
Negative: I generally mess things up.
Positive: If I mess up, I will learn from it.
Negative: I have always been like this.
Positive: I am available to change.
Negative: I will fall flat.
Positive: I need to succeed.
Negative: My life is dreadful.
Positive: I am fortunate. My life could be more terrible.
Negative: No one likes me.
Positive: I like myself.
Negative: I know nothing.
Positive: I need to learn.

For What Reason is it Great For You ?

Self-talk can improve your presentation and general prosperity. For instance, research shows self-talk can assist competitors with execution. It might assist them with perseverance or to ride out a bunch of significant burdens. Besides, positive self-talk and a more hopeful standpoint can have other medical advantages, including expanded imperativeness, more prominent life fulfillment, worked resistant capability, decreased torment, better cardiovascular wellbeing, better actual prosperity, diminished risk for death, less pressure, and misery.
It's not satisfactory why hopeful people and people with more certain self-talk experience these advantages. Notwithstanding, research proposes individuals with positive self-talk might have mental

abilities that permit them to take care of issues, think unexpectedly, and be more proficient at adapting to difficulties or difficulties. This can lessen the harmful impacts of pressure and nervousness. Positive reasoning and confidence can be powerful pressure on the executive's instruments.

To be sure, having a more uplifting perspective on life can furnish you with some medical advantages. Assuming you accept your self-talk is excessively negative, or on the other hand, if you need to underscore positive self-talk, you can figure out how to move that inward exchange. It can assist you with being a more certain individual, and it might work on your wellbeing.

How Can it Function?

Before you can figure out how to rehearse more self-talk, you should initially distinguish negative reasoning. This sort of reasoning and self-talk for the most part falls into four classifications:

- Customizing: You fault yourself for everything
- Amplifying: You center around the negative parts of a circumstance, disregarding all of the positives.
- Catastrophizing: You anticipate the most awful, and you seldom let rationale or reason convince you in any case.
- Polarizing: You see the world dressed clearly, or great and terrible. There's in the middle between and no center ground for handling and classifying life-altering situations.

At the point when you start to perceive your kinds of negative reasoning, you can attempt to transform them into positive reasoning. This errand requires practice and time and doesn't grow for the time being. Fortunately, it should be possible. Here are more instances of how to turn negative self-talk into positive self-talk

Negative: I'll frustrate everybody if I alter my perspective.

Positive: I can alter my perspective. Others will comprehend.

Negative: I fizzled and humiliated myself.

Positive: I'm glad for myself for attempting. That took mental fortitude.

Negative: I'm overweight and flabby. I should not annoy you.

Positive: I am fit in areas of strength and, I need to get better for me.

Negative: I let everybody in my group down when I didn't score.
Positive: Sports are a group occasion. We win and lose together.
Negative: I've never done this and I'll be awful at it.
Positive: This is a superb chance for me to gain from others and develop.
Negative: There's simply no chance this will work.
Positive: I can and will do the best that I can with it to make it work.

How Might you Utilize This Consistently?

Positive self-talk takes practice if it's not your regular sense. Assuming you're by and large more skeptical, you can figure out how to move your internal discourse to be seriously reassuring and inspiring. In any case, framing another propensity takes time and exertion. After some time, your contemplations can move. Positive self-talk can turn into your standard.

These tips can help:

• Recognize negative self-talk traps: Certain situations might build your self-uncertainty and lead to more bad self-talk. Work occasions, for instance, might be especially hard. Pinpointing when you experience the most regrettable self-talk can help you expect and plan.

• Check-in with your sentiments: Stop during occasions or terrible days and assess your self-talk. Is it becoming negative? How might you turn it around?

• Track down the humor: Laughter can assist with easing pressure and strain. At the point when you want a lift for positive self-talk, track down ways of giggling, like watching entertaining creature recordings or a humorist.

• Encircle yourself with positive individuals: Whether or not you notice it, you can retain the standpoint and feelings of individuals around you. This incorporates pessimistic and positive, so pick positive individuals when you can.

• Give yourself assertions: Sometimes, seeing positive words or moving pictures can be sufficient to divert your contemplations. Post little updates in your office, in your home, and any place you invest a lot of energy.

Making Improvements to Your Self-Confidence

Confidence doesn't imply that you'll constantly get everything you could want. In any case, can we just look at things objectively for a moment: How you cooperate matters. Truth be told, how you act when you convey may matter as much as and some of the time more than the words that you say. Envision somebody requesting a raise. One individual does such a cheerfully and clear look, while one more says similar words with a glare and gazes at her shoes or looks down. Your non-verbal communication and style not just influence whether you get what you need, yet additionally how you feel about yourself.

Now and again we connect in manners that lessen our self-assurance. It's fundamental to your own identity to communicate in a way that encourages you, as opposed to being defenseless. Strangely, you don't need to be sure to act certain. On account of correspondence, activities frequently go before sentiments. Act sure and you could discover that you're resting easier by thinking about yourself, too.

Ways to Seem Confident:

1. Steady and unmistakable voice tone: You might have to rehearse, yet talking in an unmistakable voice without murmurs or stammering conveys confidence.
2. Visually connecting: No gazing at the floor or glancing through the window. Certain eye-to-eye connection is not a tenacious gaze, yet it is a gathering of the eyes as you talk and come to a meaningful conclusion.
3. Paying attention to other people: Paying attention to others is an approach to growing your perspective on the world, crossing over the distinctions between you and another person, and showing that your faith in yourself is sufficiently able to take in different perspectives.
4. No Assaults or Dangers: Fearlessness isn't forceful. A confident individual can hear what somebody is talking about, answer them

and keep up with their perspective or make compromises to take care of the genuine issues that are introduced.

5. Talk from the heart: Take a stab at interfacing with your inward feeling of prosperity and your internal convictions when you converse with others and champion yourself. You could seem enthusiastic, yet enthusiasm can radiate a feeling of sureness.

6. Search for mutual benefit arrangements: At the point when you're certain, you know that getting your specific manner doesn't need to come to another person's detriment. Move toward a circumstance with the demeanor that it is conceivable that the two viewpoints are substantial and that at least two individuals can acquire from a connection.

7. Use humor: When something is crucial to us, examining it in a carefree way is hard. Yet, humor can ease pressure and show you're OK with yourself.

8. Offer Thanks: Certainty is different from self-importance. Somebody sure can offer thanks to another person. A special reward is that offering thanks is one of the best ways of reinforcing connections.

9. Apologize when off base: However not for being alive or having authentic human requirements.

10. Recognize others: Offer and get praises, and perceive others' troubles.

11. Positive contemplations can be an extremely strong method for working on fearlessness.

12. Acknowledge praises and praise yourself: When you get a commendation from another person, express gratitude toward them and request more subtleties; what precisely did they like? Perceive your accomplishments and celebrate them by remunerating yourself and informing loved ones concerning them.

13. Use analysis as an opportunity for growth: Everyone unexpectedly sees the world, according to their viewpoint, and what works for one individual may not work for another. The analysis is only the assessment of another person. Be confident while getting analysis, don't answer in a guarded way or let analysis bring down your confidence. Pay attention to the analysis and ensure that you comprehend what is being said so you can involve analysis as a method for learning and get to the next level.

14. Attempt to remain commonly happy and have an uplifting perspective on life: Possibly grumble or scrutinize when vital and, when you do, do as such in a valuable way. Offer others praises and compliment them on their triumphs.

15. Conversing with Others and Following Their Lead

16. Find yourself a certain good example: In a perfect world, this will be somebody that you see routinely, a work partner, a relative, or a companion. Someone with a ton of self-assurance who you might want to reflect on. Notice them and notice how they act when they are being certain. How would they move, how would they talk, what do they say, and when? How would they act when confronted with an issue or error? How would they communicate with others and how would others respond to them? On the off chance that conceivable converse with them to find out about how they think and what is most important to them. Addressing and being around sure individuals will ordinarily assist you with feeling more certain.

Gain from other people who are effective in satisfying the undertakings and objectives that you wish to accomplish. Let their confidence come off on you. As you become more sure then offer assistance and exhortation, become a good example for someone less confident. Confidence is infectious. The absence of certainty is as well. By and large, individuals are drawn to confident individuals, certainty is one of the principal attributes of charisma.

In some cases, the world is more impressive than us and we can't change what is happening. Notwithstanding, acting with balance, declining to offer out all that to get the endorsement, and preferring and giving admiration have the additional advantage of causing you to feel more regarded and more fearless. If you accept that you can accomplish something, you are probably going to strive to ensure you do so. Nonetheless, you don't completely accept that you can achieve an errand; you are bound to move toward it weakly and subsequently be bound to fall flat.

The stunt is persuading yourself that you can follow through with something. With the right assistance, backing, readiness, and information. Know your assets and shortcomings. Compose a rundown of things that you are great at and things that you know need improvement. Examine your rundown with loved ones as they will want to add to the rundown. Celebrate and foster your assets and track down ways of improving or dealing with your shortcomings.

Putting forth an attempt to save your relationship knowing that as people we as a whole commit errors is vital.
Try not to consider your error's negatives yet rather as learning opens doors. Put forth an attempt to save your relationship by helping yourself-self-assurance.

Experience

As we effectively complete undertakings and objectives, our certainty that we can get done with the equivalent and comparable responsibilities again increases.
A straightforward illustration of this is driving a vehicle. A great many people who have been driving for quite a while do so naturally. They don't need to ponder which pedal to push or how to deal with an intersection in the street, they take care of business. This differs from a student driver who will presumably feel anxious and need to focus hard. The student needs insight and hence trust in their capacity to drive. Acquiring experience and venturing out can, nonetheless, be truly challenging. Frequently the possibility of beginning something new is more terrible than really getting it done. This is where readiness, learning, and thinking decidedly can help.
Anything that you do, means to become as great as possible. The better you are at accomplishing something the more certain you become.

Be Assertive

Being confident means defending what you have confidence in and adhering to your standards. Being empathic likewise implies that you can alter your perspective assuming you accept it is the proper thing to do, not because you are feeling the squeeze from another person. Emphaticness, certainty, and confidence are firmly connected. As a rule, individuals become normally more confident as they foster their certainty.

Resist the Urge to Panic

There is generally a relationship among certainty and serenity. On the off chance that you have good expectations about an errand, you will probably have a quiet outlook on making it happen. At the point when you feel less certain you are bound to be focused on or anxious. Attempting to resist the urge to panic, in any event, when you're under pressure and tension, will quite often cause you to feel more sure. To do this it is helpful to figure out how to unwind.
Advance somewhere around one unwinding procedure that works for yourself and that you can utilize assuming you're feeling anxious. This might be just about as straightforward as taking a few conscious full breaths both in and out.

Keep Away From Arrogance

The presumption is hindering Communication in connections. As your confidence develops and you become fruitful, try not to feel or act better than others. Keep in mind - no one is awesome and there is in every case more that you can learn. Comment your assets and triumphs, and perceive your shortcomings and disappointments. Give others credit for their work - use praises and commendation truly. Be respectful and amiable, show an interest in the things others are doing, clarify pressing issues and reach out. Confess your slip-ups and be ready to chuckle at yourself.

CHAPTER 2: Comprehend and Develop Emotional Intelligence

The capacity to appreciate individuals on a deeper level portrays capacity, limit, expertise, or self-saw capacity to recognize, survey, and deal with the feelings of one's self, of others, and gatherings.

The hypothesis is getting a charge out of significant help in the writing and has had effective applications in numerous spaces. If your close-to-home capacities aren't close by, if you don't have mindfulness, if you can't deal with your troubling feelings, if you can't have sympathy and have powerful connections, then, at that point, regardless of how brilliant you will be, you won't get much of anywhere.

More extensive areas of knowledge empower or direct how fruitful our strength, assurance, and vision help. In any case, the capacity to understand people on a profound level, frequently estimated as an ability to understand anyone on a deeper level remainder, or EQ, is increasingly more pertinent to significant business-related results like individual execution, hierarchical efficiency, and creating individuals because its standards give a better approach to comprehend and evaluate the ways of behaving, the executive's styles, mentalities, relational abilities, and capability of individuals. It is an undeniably significant thought in human asset arranging, position profiling, enlistment talking and determination, learning and advancement, and client relations and client assistance, among others. Individuals who have a serious level of the capacity to understand people on a profound level know themselves well indeed and are likewise ready to detect the feelings of others.

By fostering their ability to appreciate anyone on a profound level people can turn out to be more useful and effective at what they do, and help other people become more useful and fruitful as well. The interaction and results of the capacity to appreciate anyone on a deeper level improvement likewise contain numerous components known to decrease pressure for people and in this manner associations by directing clash; advancing comprehension and connections; and cultivating solidness, congruity, and concordance. To wrap things up, it connects emphatically with ideas of adoration and otherworldliness.

The Model

People have various characters, needs, requirements, and approaches to showing their feelings. Exploring through this requires affability and quickness, particularly on the off chance that one desires to prevail throughout everyday life. This is where the ability to understand anyone on a deeper level hypothesis makes a difference.

In the most conventional structure, five spaces of the capacity to appreciate people on a deeper level cover together private (mindfulness, self-guideline, and self-inspiration) and social (social mindfulness and interactive abilities) skills. They are;

Mindfulness

1 Emotional mindfulness: Recognizing one's feelings and belongings.

2 Accurate self-appraisal: Knowing one's assets and cutoff points.

3 Self-certainty: Sureness around one's self-esteem and abilities.

Self-Regulation

1 Self-control: Managing troublesome feelings and motivations.

2 Trustworthiness: Maintaining principles of genuineness and respectability.

3 Conscientiousness: Taking liability regarding individual execution.

4 Adaptability: Flexibility in dealing with change.

5 Innovativeness: Being OK with and open to original thoughts and new data.

Self-Motivation

1 Achievement drive: Striving to improve or fulfill a guideline of greatness.

2 Commitment: Aligning with the objectives of the gathering or association.

3 Initiative: Readiness to follow up on open doors.

4 Optimism: Persistence in chasing after objectives notwithstanding deterrents and difficulties.

Social Awareness

1 Empathy: Sensing others' sentiments and viewpoints, and taking a functioning interest in their interests.

2 Service direction: Anticipating, perceiving, and addressing clients' requirements.

3 Developing others: Sensing what others need to create, and reinforcing their capacities.

4 Leveraging variety: Cultivating amazing open doors through different individuals.

5 Political mindfulness: Reading a gathering's flows and power connections.

Interactive abilities

1 Influence: Wielding viable strategies for influence.

2 Communication: Sending clear and persuading messages.

3 Leadership: Inspiring and directing gatherings and individuals.
4 Change impetus: Initiating or overseeing change.
5 Conflict the executives: Negotiating and settling conflicts.
6 Building bonds: Nurturing instrumental connections.
7 Collaboration and participation: Working with others toward shared objectives.
8 Team abilities: Creating a bunch of collaboration in chasing after aggregate objectives.

In a nutshell, the five spaces connect with knowing your feelings; dealing with your feelings; rousing yourself; perceiving and grasping others' feelings, and overseeing connections, i.e., dealing with the feelings of others. A typical inquiry connects with whether individuals are brought into the world with high EQ or whether it very well may be learnEd.

Truly some will be more normally gifted than others however fortunately the ability to appreciate anyone on a profound level can be mastered. (This should be so because the ability to understand individuals on a deeper level is displayed to increase with age.) However, for this to occur, individuals should be by and by propelled, practice widely what they realize, get input, and build up their new abilities.

What Emotional Intelligence Mean for Relationships

Thc ability to appreciate anyone on a deeper level (EQ) is the mystery of enduring close connections, to a great extent since it makes us very mindful of the progressions huge and little that is continually happening in ourselves as well as other people. By building your EQ, you'll have the responsiveness that every one of us is continuously looking for in a huge other.

You'll naturally detect, through dynamic mindfulness and compassion, the little changes in the elements of your sentiment that signal a requirement for activity.

We can accomplish the sort of affection we as a whole long for profound closeness, common graciousness, genuine responsibility, heartfelt caring essentially due to sympathy, and our intrinsic capacity to share close-to-home insight. Yet, to arrive at the level of sentiment we want every one of the abilities of a high EQ: sharp profound attention to abstain from confusing fixation or desire with enduring adoration, acknowledgment to encounter feelings that could hurt a relationship whenever left to rot, and watchful dynamic attention to evaluate us of what's working and what isn't.

Fabricating Genuinely Insightful Heartfelt Communications

We don't need to pick some unacceptable sweethearts, end up in different bombed relationships, or let the sentiment leak out of our drawn-out connections. We don't need to let clashing requirements and needs to interfere with two individuals who love one another.

We don't need to surrender to fatigue or squabbling in our adoration lives. We can achieve the sort of adoration we as a whole long for profound closeness and common generosity, genuine commitment, and heartfelt caring were given compassion and our natural capacity to share the profound experience. Yet, to accomplish those relationship objectives, we want every one of the abilities of a high EQ:

- Insightful close-to-home attention to abstain from confusing captivation or desire with enduring adoration
- Acknowledgment to encounter feelings that could hurt a relationship whenever left to rot, and
- Cautious dynamic attention to inform us about what's working and what isn't.

Luckily, your EQ doesn't have to have crested before you set out on adoration. As a matter of fact, for some individuals, falling head over heels fills in as inspiration for reconstructing the heart. That is the reason the absolute most profoundly energetic darlings are in their eighties. They find that two high EQs amount to a sentiment that grows constantly, never loses energy, and consistently fortifies them both, independently as well as on the whole.

Effectively Look for Change in Your Relationship

At the point when you brave your feeling of dread toward change, you find that various things don't necessarily mean more awful things frequently come out over and above anyone's expectations on the furthest side of progress. Connections are organic entities themselves, and ordinarily should change. Any connections not prodded toward the sort of development you need will float into change of another sort perhaps one you don't need.

Your capacity to embrace change takes care of fortitude and hopefulness. Ask yourself, does your darling need a genuinely new thing from you? Do you have to plan a chance to reexamine together? Are outside impacts requesting an adjustment of your individual jobs? Is it true that you are all around as cheerful as you used to be? Without EQ, such inquiries are frequently too terrifying to even think about confronting, such countless sweethearts overlook signs of progress until it's past the point of no return.

View the difficulties you experience as any open doors instead of issues. Your mental fortitude and positive thinking permit you to see predicaments not as issues, but rather as trying to open doors. How innovative might you two at any point be? At the point when you don't have to fault each other for your feelings, you're not constrained by pessimistic close to home recollections, and you're ready not to rehash the standard, worn out botch. At the point when you have a high EQ, you're freed from grooves and renunciation, and you can get down to creative critical thinking. You can meet contrasts among you and inescapable emergencies, as solicitations to see as one another, difficulties to draw nearer and arise independently and by and large more grounded.

Regard Every one of the Sentiments you Have for one Another

We're not generally pleased by the revelations we make about the individual we love, yet with regards to feelings, tolerating them all is important. Being infatuated doesn't mean never feeling furious, disheartened, hurt, or envious. How you follow up on your feelings depends on you; what's significant is that you really feel them. Numerous connections have been destroyed by fault, and a huge number of couples have passed up profound closeness in view of disgrace. Both are awful remnants of unfelt outrage, dread, and nervousness. In the event that you've accomplished by building EQ, you'll encounter the feelings and move on together.

Keep the Giggling in Your Love Life

To stay away from intellectualizing feelings you really want acknowledgment, and a major piece of your acknowledgment comes from chuckling. Sweethearts who can't giggle together about themselves presumably aren't extremely tolerating of their connections. They will be unable to endure its interesting defects and inescapable staggers, anything else than they can tolerate on their own. They're likewise less inclined to be available to a relationship's most unexpected, yet wonderful treats. Your high EQ, interestingly, implies you can continue to work on your relationship, however you won't ever get caught by narrow minded assumptions for flawlessness.

Focus on how you Feel When Your Sweetheart Isn't Anywhere Near

Luckily, you have a perfect approach to checking precisely the way in which your relationship is going. Utilize the three measures of prosperity to sort out how the remainder of your life is going. Might it be said that you are feeling fretful or crabby overall? Do you haul during your time at the workplace or school following an evening of conjugal delight? Do you disdain loved ones despite the fact that you two are spending each accessible moment alone together? Love never profits by limited focus. In the event that you don't feel fiery,

perceptive, and big-hearted constantly, it doesn't exactly make any difference whether you coo like birds when you're together.
On the off chance that the sex couldn't be better however you're slipping working, assuming you have a solid sense of security and comfortable hearing "Hello, honey" when you get back home around evening time yet are experiencing difficulty getting up in the first part of the day, something's not right despite the fact that all that feels warm and fluffy in the palace. At the point when this occurs, all the data about you, your darling, and your relationship that your feelings and your keenness have assembled will control you to the best arrangement.

Fostering Your Self-Confidence Skills

Self-assurance can decrease over the long run in the event that you don't rehearse your abilities or on the other hand assuming you hit set-backs. As you become more self-assured you ought to keep on rehearsing your abilities to keep up with and help your confidence further. Setting your self-confidence focuses on expecting you to get out of your usual range of familiarity and do things that cause you to feel a level of anxiety or dread.
Potential confidence targets might include;
1. Begin an undertaking or task that you've been investing in for a long time: Frequently we put off beginning significant assignments since they appear to be overpowering, troublesome or abnormal to finish. Just creating a beginning on such an undertaking can support confidence and make you more leaned to finish it.
2. Submit a question in an eatery in the event that there is an issue with your request: On the off chance that you wouldn't for the most part gripe about an issue then, at that point, doing so is an effective method for working on your confidence and emphaticness abilities.
3. Stand up and pose an inquiry at a public gathering or in a gathering: By doing this you are making yourself the focal point of consideration for a couple of moments.
4. Volunteer to give a show or deliver a speech: For some individuals addressing a gathering is an especially startling

possibility. The most effective way to defeat this apprehension and gain confidence is with experience.

5. Acquaint yourself with another person: This could be some place where individuals share something for all intents and purposes, like at a party or a meeting, making it possibly simpler to have a discussion. Or on the other hand you could converse with a total outsider in a lift/lift.

6. Wear something that will draw attention: Like an ostentatious variety. Individual appearance is a significant consideration and individuals with lower confidence will quite often make an effort not to be taken note. Say something and captivate everyone.

7. Join a gathering or class locally. You will possibly help in loads of various ways by meeting new neighborhood individuals and learning new things while working on your certainty.

8. Take a new excursion on an open vehicle: Going to another spot utilizing a new course and with arbitrary individuals will cause the vast majority to feel marginally awkward.

What is your opinion about every one of the thoughts on the rundown above? Maybe some gave you minor sensations of butterflies while others filled you with fear. Albeit the rundown utilizes normal instances of possible confidence supporting undertakings none might be appropriate for you. Think about some confidence that is ideal for you, then, at that point, begin with simpler ones and develop.

CHAPTER 3: Being Authentic

What might be your response when you find that your accomplice has been claiming to be who they were not? For certain individuals, it would make them extremely upset to discover that they have been in a situation that doesn't satisfy their fantasies about supporting bona fide connections. One reason why individuals set up an organized form of themselves prior to entering a relationship is on the grounds that they are anxious about the possibility that their accomplice will not acknowledge them.

Being consistent with yourself in a relationship could sound startling, however it fabricates veritable closeness and love. Bona fide connections are organized to endure for an extremely long period in light of the fact that the two accomplices are prepared to share the general mishmash sides of themselves without dread or favor.

What's the Significance Here in Connections?

Legitimacy in connections happens when the two players tell the truth and are authentic with one another. The two accomplices comprehend that nobody is great, yet they will acknowledge each other's defects and come to a productive and positive split. All the more significantly, it concentrates on showing that vagueness in connections is one method for fostering a real connection between two accomplices. Besides, true connections are absent any and all trepidation and uncertainty in light of the fact that the two life partners love each other sincerely, in any event, while imparting their weakness.

Showing legitimacy is an essential part of a relationship. In the event that you are consistent with yourself in a relationship and your accomplice follows after accordingly, it turns into a sound, solid, and fair relationship. To foster this quality and keep up with legitimate connections, here are far to begin:

1. Deliberate and Chivalrous Communication:

Being purposeful and obliging while conveying causes your accomplicc to understand that you care about their sentiments. At the point when your accomplice specifies their necessities to you, it is fundamental not to make it about yourself all things considered. With regards to the demonstration of being authentic, deliberate, and obliging, correspondence is one of the essential measuring sticks for estimation. It is critical to specify that this sort of correspondence is a two-way street, as it includes talking, tuning in, and investing quality energy figuring out the other individual's viewpoints.

2. Decide to Cherish Your Partner Everyday:

Cherishing your partner is indispensable to turning into a valid individual. It is convenient to express that a partner who chooses to adore effectively and intentionally is bound to have more fruitful connections than people who don't. It might be ideal on the off chance that you were conscious of the way you act and address your accomplice. Assuming you let your accomplice know that you love and care about them, it ought to likewise reflect in how you help and towards them. All things considered, activities in all actuality do express stronger than words. Deciding to cherish your accomplice consistently assists you with regarding them as fundamentally important. Your companion will have a real sense of safety since you love them purposely, and they can see it in your activities. Ordinary activities assist with making a credible association as couples figure out how to trust one another.

3. Make Limits in Your Relationship:

Couples need to make limits and make a deal to avoid crossing them to be consistent with themselves. There are a few things that you could do without that would be excruciating to you when your accomplice does them. Despite seeing someone, you have your uniqueness, and you shouldn't think twice about it. It is fundamental to put down stopping points since much harm should be possible to the relationship when those lines are crossed. Regarding limits includes regarding and confiding in one another and choosing not to harm the relationship by accomplishing something deliberately that harms your accomplice.

4. Be Straightforward:

Many individuals view it troublesome as straightforward in connections since they can't bear the possibility of having their accomplice know a few mysteries about them. Credible connections are based on straightforwardness because the two players will be focused on discussing their thoughts, thoughts, and acts without concealing anything. Being straightforward with your companion involves sharing things you generally have a humiliating outlook on while offering them to any other person. You will be uncovering your weaknesses, yet you are laying out realness over the long haul.

5. Learn and Rehearse Each Other's Main Avenues for Affection:

There are five general ways by which heartfelt companions express love to one another. These five dialects are Physical Touch, Acts of administration, Quality time, Words of insistence, and Giving gifts. To be legitimate in seeing someone, you should gain proficiency with your accomplice's ways to express affection truly. Having this information assists you with adoring them in the manner they want to be cherished. Then again, choosing not to know your accomplice's ways to express affection could recommend that you are not deliberate about being in a genuine relationship.

6. Try not to Allow Your Relationship to be the Sole Wellspring of Your Joy:

Nobody must be forced into permitting their relationship to be the main wellspring of their satisfaction. Before the relationship, you got your delight from different means. Also, even though you need to make a few changes in the relationship, losing your identity is significant not. To foster legitimacy, you need to adjust your relationship and different parts of your life. Your relationship ought to be one of the many wellsprings of your joy and by all accounts, not the only source. By discrediting yourself over and over, disdain and scorn can begin saturating the elements with your accomplice. In a genuine relationship, the two accomplices hold their feeling of personality even though they are enamored, and they don't utilize control to keep each other cheerful. At the point when you pursue accomplishing your objectives and developing your advantage, you will find satisfaction in the thing you are doing, and it will help the relationship as well.

7. Face the Difficulties as Opposed to Keeping Away From Them:

Challenges are unavoidable, and the most effective way to win is by handling them as opposed to keeping away from them. In valid connections, challenges happen, and the two accomplices can move beyond these issues since they see each other back to the front. They arrive at a degree of mindfulness and veritable closeness that permits them to take care of any issue that they are looking for easily. Furthermore, they likewise understand that their relationship has turned into a significant device in helping their self-awareness.

8. Treasure each second with your accomplice

To lay out a veritable association, you must be cognizant and vital. It is vital to invest adequate energy in sharing your objectives, aspirations, sentiments, and contemplations with your accomplice. Quality time together can assist your joining forces with seeing the genuine you and having a superior comprehension of what your identity is. Value such minutes since they will end up being pivotal occasions for the relationship. In true connections, the two accomplices invest adequate energy in having top to bottom conversations that assist them with figuring out their accomplice more. Furthermore, they make time to have some good times and unwind because it makes them bond better.

9. Get a Sense of Ownership With Your Activities:

Genuine connections can't stand the test of time on the off chance that you keep on faulting your companion for your off-base activities. Tragically, certain individuals avoid tolerating their decisions since they would rather not live with their missteps. Thus, they like to accuse another person, imagining that it will help them. On the off chance that you keep on staying away from liability as opposed to considering yourself responsible, you're not creating credibility, and the relationship could keep on anguish. It is crucial to significantly impact your attitude and adapt to the situation by tracking down arrangements contingent upon your accomplice for help.

10. Value Your Relationship:

It is important to specify that legitimate connections are a result of mates who treasure their relationship and do all that could be within reach to keep it working. Smugness breeds cynicism and frailty in any relationship, and along these lines, endeavors ought to be made consistently to stay away from that. Concentrates on led-on couples in long haul personal connections have plainly shown an immediate relationship between genuineness seeing someone and heartfelt connection, alongside providing care to an accomplice. You ought to be seeing someone for the right reasons since it decides how much worth you put on it and your accomplice. A genuine relationship gives the open door for you and your life partner to value each other despite the chances.

CHAPTER 4

Communication is the reason for a sound marriage. It's the way you and your life partner associate, share your contemplations and perspectives, and resolve questions. Relationship relational abilities don't come simply for everybody. A few couples should deal with their methods for a long time. However, over the long run, they will want to talk transparently and genuinely with each other. Regardless of how associated you and your life partner are currently, there is dependably space to fortify and develop your relationship.

The Following are 10 Relationship Correspondences Abilities That will Save Your Marriage:

1. Genuinely Focus on Your Accomplice:

Don't text and talk. Whether your companion is making you a quip or uncovering a profound special kind of mystery, you ought to be intently focusing on them. Set aside diverting innovation, quiet or mood killer the TV, and incline in towards your accomplice. This will show them you care about their data. Gesturing and keeping in touch are both great approaches to showing your accomplice you are tuning in. You can make a spot in your home where the gadgets can be set to restrict mechanical interruptions.

2. Try not to interfere with your accomplice:

Being interfered with is the fastest method for raising a contention. While speaking with your accomplice, the two players must feel they get an opportunity to talk and to be heard. It might feel enticing to press as you would see it while your accomplice is still talking, particularly if you feel they entirely misunderstand a reality, however it means a lot to stand by. Focusing on your accomplice while remaining on track and associated shows your accomplice regard. Try not to interfere with your accomplice

3. Make an impartial space:

It is generally difficult to Communicate. Many couples find it useful to handle "extreme" military subjects in an unbiased space, for example, the kitchen table. It might sound senseless, yet examining your accomplice's absence of sexual ability while in bed can cause them to feel went after and can make them view the room in a negative light from now on. Contending at an overall home is one more illustration of one accomplice feeling like they have the so-called "strategic position" in the contention.

4. Talk eye to eye:

One of the most amazing relational abilities in connections you can utilize is continuously talking about significant subjects up close and personal. Messaging is positively not the road to having serious relationship discussions or pursuing enormous choices since the manner of speaking is not entirely settled through instant messages. All things considered, pick when you can be up close and personal with your accomplice. This way you could both offer each other your full consideration and you at any point can peruse each other's non-verbal signs. At the point when things are said face to face, there is no place for things to get "lost in interpretation" through tech. Talk up close and personal with your partner.

5. Use "I" explanations when issues emerge:

One issue couples run into when they are contending is going after one another. By utilizing "I" explanations, you ease the heat off your accomplice. Rather than saying "YOU did this and it drove me crazy", have a go at conveying "I feel that when THIS happened, my sentiments were harmed." See the distinction? You made the issue your own, rather than going after your accomplice. This straightforward, yet compelling procedure forestalls both of you from going into assault mode or turning out to be unnecessarily protective with each other.

6. Be straightforward with your life partner:

Being straightforward is generally difficult, however, it is the way into a sound relationship. One investigation discovered that great correspondence, genuineness, and trust were recorded as probably the best calibers. Being straightforward means letting your accomplice know when you feel some issues should be discussed. It additionally implies conceding when you were off-base and saying 'sorry' as opposed to rationalizing. Besides the fact that genuineness helps cultivate authentic open correspondence among you and your mate, it additionally assists work with trust.

7. Discuss the easily overlooked details:

One of the extraordinary relational abilities in connections is the point at which you and your accomplice can discuss the easily overlooked details as well as the enormous things. You can reinforce your marriage by discussing your day, and your contemplations, or offering interesting stories from your week. At the point when you are hitched, each subject ought to be open for conversation. There ought not to be whatever is excessively off-kilter or awkward to share. By discussing the easily overlooked details you will make it simpler to discuss more significant points from now on.

8. Utilize the 24-hour-rule:

At the point when two individuals are hitched and living respectively, there will undoubtedly be obstacles. Every so often you will feel like rainbows and butterflies float through your home when your accomplice is close. At different times, you'll feel a migraine coming on when your companion is close. On the off chance that you are feeling disappointed with your accomplice and are going to voice your grumbling, stop briefly. Practice the 24-hour rule. So she didn't void the dishwasher or he didn't get his socks. Is it the apocalypse? Will it make a difference to you in 24 hours? If not, consider letting it go.

9. Connect:

Regardless of what tone your discussion is taking, actual contact is significant. The low-force feeling of the skin, like contacting an accomplice or stroking their arm, advances the arrival of oxytocin. The affection chemical advances holding and sympathy in significant others, and it can likewise go about as an enemy of stress specialists and advances a helpful way of behaving.

10. Make correspondence fun:

Conveying is how you discuss family and monetary issues, issues, and their answers, and how you and your companion simply decide. However, remember that conveying ought to be fun, as well. Chatting with your accomplice implies sharing amusing stories, dreams for the future, and partaking in profound discussion. These are the minutes that make a more profound close-to-home association and lift oxytocin and dopamine. Continuously make time to check in with your life partner verbally, whether the discussion that follows is significant or senseless.

6 Ways To Communicate Better in Your Relationships

1. Pose Receptive Inquiries:

Communication isn't just about discussing each other's days and getting out whatever you need to have for lunch. It's tied in with having the option to dig profoundly and get to know this individual as well as you can. It's not generally simple to dig profoundly, particularly for people who have never been open to discussing their sentiments.

Furthermore, making each discussion a heart-to-heart is excessive. There are ways of doing this without forcing your life partner to spill their most profound mysteries. For instance, rather than posing yes or no inquiries like "Did you have a decent day?" take a stab at posing more unassuming inquiries like, "How was your day?" Yes, they might answer with a brief non-answer ("great", "fine", "something similar"), yet posing unconditional inquiries offers them a chance to share more if they decide to.

Remember that not every person opens up without any problem. Show restraint toward your accomplice if they are not sharing constantly. We put down stopping points around our feelings and everybody's limits are unique. In this way, be careful and deferential of their close-to-home limits, and they ought to be similarly careful and conscious of yours.

Eventually, the more you get to know your life partner on a more profound level, the more transparent you might be with one another. What's more, genuineness breeds trust, which are two vital mainstays of a solid relationship (here's a clue: communication is another very significant point of support!).

2. Get on Nonverbal Cues:

Assuming your accomplice says "my day was fine" however their tone sounds disturbed, upset, or irate, then, at that point, there might be something different that they're not yet prepared to convey. Communication isn't just about the words we say yet additionally the way that we say them. Our tone and our disposition offer much something beyond the words emerging from our mouths. Furthermore, it's an expertise to have the option to get on those nonverbal signs. Check your spouse's looks, their hands (would they say they are shuddering/restless?), their non-verbal communication (Are they visually connecting out? Are they folding their arms?), and pay attention to their manner of speaking.

3. Try not to Try to Read Their Mind:

Now and again you can tell by simply checking out at somebody what they might feel. Doing this and can we just be real: however much we need to be clairvoyants, we aren't and shouldn't need to be is difficult all of the time. Along these lines, if you don't know what your accomplice is feeling, ask them. If you're the one holding things in and anticipating that your accomplice should guess what you might be thinking, pause for a minute to see the value in the way that your accomplice is trying by asking you what's happening as opposed to disregarding the issue.

Give your all to tell them how you're feeling when you're prepared to get serious about it. It's not beneficial to say you're alright when you're not and afterward fly off the handle at your accomplice for not sorting it out. Speak the truth about how you feel as well as could be expected, and attempt to communicate it solidly before it reaches the place where it explodes and somebody says something they lament. Being immediate is in every case better compared to being latent forceful.

Assuming your partner is the person who is at fault for being inactive and forceful, take a stab at telling them that it's somewhat terrible for both of you when they're not legitimate about how they feel. Obviously, it's wonderful when we realize each other so well that we can essentially peruse each other's contemplations and know the precisely exact thing to say in the right minutes, yet we're human and we might commit errors once in a while or miss prompts that appear glaringly evident to our accomplice or the other way around. You both must try to all the more likely see one another and show restraint toward one another, as well.

4. Discussions are a Two-Way Street:

As you speak with your accomplice observe how frequently you say "I", "You", or "We". If the discussion is for the most part about yourself, it's not exactly a discussion. Make sure to turn it back to your mate and pose inquiries about how they feel, what their contemplations are, and what's the deal with them. If you observe that you're not kidding a great deal, what's the unique situation? Could it be said that you are pointing fingers and finding fault? Connections are about two individuals, and each ought to have an equivalent expression about things. The two individuals need to feel appreciated and have the option to share what's at the forefront of their thoughts. If you feel like your accomplice is the one overwhelming the discussions and you can't get a word in that frame of mind, tell them this. They may not know that they're overwhelming the discussion. Discussions resemble a tennis match; it ought to stream normally this way and that to every individual.

5. Put Away the Opportunity to Talk:

My accomplice and I as of late moved in together and we were cautioned by basically everybody that it's a "represent the moment of truth" circumstance for couples. We were apprehensive, however, we both had a presumptuous mentality of 'we got this. We have forever been perfect at conveying straightforwardly and genuinely with one another. We had no clue about how living respectively would fundamentally impact how we needed to convey, yet it positively did. During the initial three weeks together, we quibbled continually. We were so irritated about the quibbling (as opposed to what we were quarreling about), that we wound up squabbling about the way that we were squabbling! Have a migraine yet? That's right, we had one for around three weeks in a row. Since we are not to the point that few, we at last plunked down and worked it out.

We needed to become familiar with a better approach to being with one another since we were currently having a similar space. We discussed the things that made a difference (like how to spend our cash) and the things that at last didn't make any difference (who makes a garbage run). Discussing those things was significant because we couldn't have ever realized what made a difference to the next individual had we not plunked down to examine it.

At last, we discovered that none of our squabblings was about the genuine things we were quarreling over, but instead, it was about not feeling appreciated or appreciated. From that day on, we chose to have what we call "Bae Sesh", a week-by-week meeting where we put away an hour to express our real thoughts in a sans judgment space. This permits us to feel appreciated and regarded. Our drawn-out "Bae Sesh" may not work for everybody, but rather it certainly works for us. We've had the option to stay away from bigger contentions, effectively pay attention to one another, and bond and feel nearer to one another due to our Bae Sessions. We might talk consistently, yet with the two of us being so occupied with work and life it's ideal to carve out an opportunity for something somewhat more profound.

6. Let Them Know What You Need From Them:

Once in a while, I simply need to vent and feel approved by having my accomplice support me by saying, "Definitely that truly sucks I'm heartbroken!" Other times, I need exhortation. Like I said previously, not even one of us are clairvoyants, so it means quite a bit to attempt to keep your accomplice informed so that you're in total agreement. Offering something ahead of time like, "I want to vent the present moment and I'm not searching for any guidance, simply your help," or, "I truly need your recommendation on this present circumstance," will tell them precisely what you want at that time. Being immediate about what you want can reduce a portion of the miscommunication or stress in a given circumstance, as well. By telling them early, we can perhaps forestall those superfluous conflicts welcomed on by miscommunication.

CHAPTER 5: Body Language

Significance of Smiling

Smiles are essential to lessen pressure and guarantee better correspondence, "A smile is the initial segment of one's non-verbal communication. It has various inflections like love, mockery, and graciousness. It likewise assists to loosen things up between two individuals and assists with advancing communication. When we smile, we signal our neighborliness, receptiveness to drawing in, and interest in individuals. A smile isn't significant for the people around you getting it, yet in addition for you. It's anything but mysterious that when you smile you feel improved, even though it tends to be somewhat troublesome toward the beginning, however at that point it is intriguing how the impact can be infectious.

Simply one more tip: look at your smile before the mirror. Here and there we imagine that we are smiling, yet we are not, so further developing our mindfulness is significant. Practice likewise a phony smile, a pleasant smile, a blissful smile... and use them to further develop your communication style!

The Significance of Eye-to-eye Connection in Communication

Visually connecting isn't simply all of the time. It can feel off-kilter on occasion, particularly when you haven't yet fabricated a bond with the other individual. In any case, why is eye-to-eye connection significant in any case? How about we reveal why eye-to-eye connection matters and how you might further develop your eye-to-

eye connection abilities? Eye-to-eye connection is a significant piece of correspondence.
In any case, to comprehend the reason why we should initially respond to a significant inquiry. Contact's meaning could be a little clearer. Eye-to-eye connection happens when two individuals check out at one another's eyes simultaneously. This is a type of nonverbal correspondence that people use to impart many types of feelings. Dissimilar to different primates, we can undoubtedly see where people are looking as a direct result of how much white encompasses our irises. Thus, we know where somebody is looking in any event, when their head doesn't move. To this end eye to eye, connection assumes a tremendous part in correspondence.
How about we investigate four motivations behind why eye-to-eye connection correspondence is significant:
1. Bond With Others:
Research has shown that eye-to-eye connection initiates the limbic mirror framework. This implies that the very neurons that are terminating in somebody's cerebrum will likewise fire in yours when you share an eye-to-eye connection with them. In this way, if their eyes are imparting bliss, neurons on your end will likewise fire to feel satisfaction. This sharing of profound states can assist you with holding with others and increment compassion between people. Two companions holding together-why-is-eye to eye connection significant
2. Show Trustworthiness:
Great eye-to-eye connection is a significant showcase of genuineness during a discussion. The eyes are a focal piece of nonverbal correspondence. They show a scope of feelings that words will not necessarily in every case talk about. What's more, genuineness can assist two individuals with building trust.
3. Increase Your Protection From the Influence:
Research has shown that immediate eye-to-eye connection can make you more impervious to influence and impact strategies. You can utilize this nonverbal prompt to be more mindful of others' impact on you.
4. Work on Understanding Between Individuals:
It's not difficult to have mistaken assumptions, in any event, when two individuals accept they're both listening eagerly. Visually connecting assists the two individuals with zeroing in on the

discussion and reading looks. This can further develop understanding and further developing comprehension can altogether further develop correspondence between two individuals.

5. Assemble Regard:

At long last, visually connecting shows and gains appreciation. It takes more than eye-to-eye connection alone to support regard in a relationship. Be that as it may, it assumes a significant part. Looking at somebody without flinching shows them that you think they are significant. Eye-to-eye connection is advantageous for the reasons we referenced above, however, different realities make it an intriguing and significant idea. We should investigate three of them:

1. Eye-to-eye Connection Helps Other People Recollect What you Said

At the point when you share an eye-to-eye connection during a discussion, you'll recall a greater amount of what the other individual said. The opposite is valid also. Others will hold a greater amount of what you said.

2. Eye-to-eye Connection can Assist With Mindfulness

Being mindful implies that you know about what's now occurring with your body. Also, eye-to-eye connection can assist with that, research observed that individuals are more mindful while they're visually connecting than while they're keeping away from the eye-to-eye connection.

3. Eye-to-eye Connection Makes Fascination

Eye-to-eye connection fascination is a genuine article. Research shows that people find others more alluring when they visually engage. Grinning can likewise assist with making fascination. While this is significant for individual connections, it additionally matters at work. Associates and pioneers will be more disposed to construct associations with you when you look at them without flinching. Then again, no eye-to-eye connection can show an absence of confidence.

Ways to Visually Engage

Assuming you find that your eyes stray from the other individual's eyes during social associations, or then again assuming you have social uneasiness, the following are five hints you can use to improve and visually engage on a more regular basis. You'll likewise figure out how to keep in touch during a whole discussion.

1. Visually Connect Before you Begin Talking:

Before you utter your most memorable word, visually engage. At the point when the contract is laid out, you can begin talking eye to eye.

2. Maintain Eye Contact for 4 to 5 Seconds all at Once:

Not certain how long you ought to maintain eye contact with someone else or how much eye-to-eye connection to make? Take a stab at investigating individuals' eyes for four to five seconds all at once. Rather than peering down when you look away, focus on the side. Then, at that point, you can continue the eye-to-eye connection.

3. Use Signals:

At any point do you feel awkward and need to look away? Rather than simply turning away, take a stab at utilizing motions and non-verbal communication. You can gesture, utilize your hands, or utilize different motions that you normally make during a discussion. This will look more normal than simply turning away.

4. Move Your Eyes Gradually:

Try not to turn away excessively fast when you look away. This can cause you to appear to be apprehensive. All things being equal, turn away leisurely.

5. Keep in Touch Half of the Time:

While you're having a conversation with somebody, utilize the 50/70 rule. This implies you ought to hold an eye-to-eye connection between half 70% of the time. Keep in touch both while you are talking and keep in mind that you are tuning in. Eye-to-eye connections can assist you with working on your connections. It can likewise assist you with expanding admiration and trust at work.

The Most Effective Method to Oversee Looks

Looks incorporate grinning, grimacing, eye-rolling, visually connecting, glaring, and seeming exhausted or intrigued. Other looks could show fervor or even shock, such as waking up or mouth generally. Winking could flag that we're kidding about a comment we made, or in any event, playing with the individual to whom we are talking! Also, causing a commotion could imply that we're shocked or that we don't completely accept what we're hearing. The translations relegated to looks shift enormously, so we should be cautious while utilizing them. A considerable lot of our demeanors are ones we're familiar with from our own social, familial, and business foundations and encounters. Since we comprehend looks unexpectedly, we can without much of a stretch get the aim behind such nonverbal signs wrong.

What you say when you impart starts some time before you open your mouth, and go on after you've completed the process of talking. The human face is incredibly expressive - ready to convey innumerable feelings without saying a word. Furthermore, dissimilar to certain types of nonverbal correspondence, the feelings shared through looks are all-inclusive. Watch somebody perusing the paper or taking a gander at their telephone, you could undoubtedly make presumptions about their inclinations toward the subject on the opposite end.

Do they concur, differ or feel energy or misery? Our face, both intentionally and automatically passes feeling and some of it is challenging to stow away. This compulsory informing frequently turns into a hindrance to our planned message and might now and again be in struggle with our expressed word. Speakeasy Instructors pinpoint two parts of looks to consider for more prominent command over our correspondence: miniature articulations and your regular scope of shown feelings.

Miniature articulations are brief, compulsory looks that normally happen in high-stake, distressing circumstances. They happen when an individual is intentionally attempting to disguise how they are feeling, or when an individual doesn't deliberately have the foggiest idea of how they are feeling. What's more, not normal for ordinary looks, they are beyond difficult to stow away. Understanding what your looks can convey is a certain something yet figuring out how to utilize them for your potential benefit is another.

Search for feeling on the essences of others, figure out how to perceive what their looks impart to you, and afterward work on coupling those articulations with the words and feelings you need to convey. Watch your number one Netflix film on quiet and you'll be flabbergasted by the amount you can follow from the non-verbal pieces of information given by your character's looks. Since we aren't all Hollywood entertainers, a few of us need to work harder to show more than our meager few "go-to" feelings. Utilize your telephone to rehearse and don't fear embellishment in some measure in the first place. Record yourself and afterward attempt to control your underlying distress, watch it without the volume. What appears to be senseless to the inward you are logical not even close as stunning when you play the clasp back on the quiet. The key likewise with all communication is to be valid. Understand what you need to convey, have faith in your position and perspective, and afterward… convey, with your words and with your face.

Like some other specialized devices, utilizing look takes trial and error, practice, and work. Contemplating the trifecta of looks joined with smart substance and bona fide conveyance will move your discussions past straightforward correspondence to building a genuine association with individuals generally critical to you.

Significance of Gesture

At the point when speakers talk, they motion. The objective of this section is to comprehend the commitment that these signals make to how we impart and think. A signal can assume a part in correspondence and think at numerous time frames. We investigate, thus, signal's commitment to how language is delivered and figured out at the time; its commitment to how we acquire language and other mental abilities; and its commitment to how language is made over ages, over adolescence, and on the spot. We find that the signals speakers produce when they talk are necessary to correspondence and can be tackled in various ways;

1. Motion mirrors speakers' contemplations, frequently their implicit considerations, and subsequently can act as a window onto discernment. Empowering speakers to signal can hence give one more course to instructors, clinicians, questioners, and so on, to all the more likely to comprehend their correspondence accomplices.
2. Signals can change speakers' considerations. Empowering motion in this way can change how understudies, patients, witnesses, and so forth, contemplate an issue and, thus, modify the direction of learning, treatment, or exchange.
3. Motion gives building blocks that can be utilized to develop a language. By seeing how youngsters and grown-ups who don't as of now have a language assembled those blocks, we can notice the

course of language creation directly. Our hands are with us Annual survey of brain research

Having Good Posture

Stance can reflect feelings, perspectives, and goals. Research has distinguished a great many postural signs and their implications, for example,

Open and Closed Posture:

Two types of stance have been distinguished, 'open' and 'shut', which might mirror a singular's level of certainty, status, or receptivity to someone else. Somebody situated in a shut position could have his/her arms collapsed, legs crossed, or be situated at a slight point from the individual with whom they are connecting. In an open stance, you could hope to see somebody straightforwardly confronting you with hands separated from the arms of the seat. An open stance can be utilized to convey receptiveness or interest in somebody and status to tune in, while the shut stance could suggest uneasiness or lack of engagement.

Continuously pay Attention

It may very well be trying to have discussions with individuals who don't share our perspectives or who see the world uniquely in contrast to us. Be that as it may, in these discussions, we can frequently permit space for different bits of insight, and having open discussions can help us learn and develop.

Ways of Having Open Exchanges, Regardless of who you are Taking to

Listen First, Talk Second:

You can relax, any one of us could be to blame for it: listening barely enough with the goal that we can plan our reaction. While we might have the option to pull off this, for the time being, it's vital to truly pay attention to one another. At the end of the day, pay attention to comprehending, not answering. Take a stab at returning to a stage to truly pay attention to the individual you're discussing with. Seek clarification on pressing issues and explain what you hear. Show interest in the things they're saying and welcome them to share more. Offering individuals our unified consideration assists us with turning out to be better communicators and causes them to feel appreciated. At the point when it's your chance to talk, request them to do likewise for you. It might take some training, however, it'll be justified eventually.

Move Toward the Discussion With a Receptive Outlook:

Move toward discussions with sympathy and understanding. It's not unexpected to have clashing sentiments when you disagree with an individual's perspective, however, it doesn't mean you can't relate to or approve of their point of view. It's additionally essential to remember that your friends probably have various reasons propelling their perspectives and activities. Attempt to comprehend what is vital to them, what they need, and how that influences their ways of behaving. Try not to make suspicions and on second thought, consider their viewpoint and educational encounters. Having significant discussions can give you a chance to get familiar with your friends and their activities.

Utilize Powerful Relational Abilities:

Having great relational abilities can assist with coordinating the discussion in a solid manner. Here are some interesting points while chatting with somebody with an alternate point of view than yours. Be careful. In some cases your enthusiasm for a point can raise unmistakable inclinations, so it is critical to be aware of your tone and disposition. Recall that it's not generally about what you say yet the way in which you say it. Check in and ask yourself "does this actually feel like a discussion or does it seem like a contention?"

Pose Unassuming Inquiries:

Questions that could go either way are questions that can't be responded to with a straightforward yes or no. These inquiries can assist with drawing out thoughts or considerations from a companion or friend. Use them as a method for acquiring further getting it, yet use them sparingly. Posing an excessive number of inquiries can cause the discussion to start to feel more like a cross examination.

Use Confirmations:

Regardless of whether you concur with somebody's situation, it means quite a bit to utilize insistences to feature the qualities and values that somebody is bringing to the discussion. Approve how they're feeling, instead of how they're acting. You can be understanding that somebody is vexed, furious or stressed, without saying it's OK to shout.

Use Reflections to Explain:

Reflections are an extraordinary specialized instrument, however they can take some training. Reflections allow us an opportunity to state back what we think somebody is hearing or talking about. This either affirms to somebody that we are hearing what they are talking about or offers them the chance to address any misinterpretations.

Sum up the Discussion:

Wrap up the discussion, or a piece of the discussion, by summing up to feature the positive parts of what you examined. Toward the finish of the discussion, thank the individual for their time and let them know that you value their readiness to talk with you.

CONCLUSION

Communication is the way into a cheerful, solid relationship. You can work on your communication in marriage by being transparent about your physical and close to home necessities, staying an open book in regards to cash matters, and really focusing on your accomplice.

Lastly, communication is an expertise, and that implies there's a consistent opportunity to get better. Cooperate with your accomplice to sort out how you can keep up with sound communication and remain in total agreement. Be as fair, immediate, kind, and insightful as you can. Whether it's with a Bae Sesh, or just putting forth a greater attempt to open dependent upon one another.

A significant number of us speak with individuals each day, whether face to face or on the incalculable computerized stages accessible to us. Be that as it may, what amount of our communication really contacts the target group or individual the manner in which we trusted? Successful communication expects us to be honest and complete in the thing we are attempting to communicate.

Try not to worry in light of the fact that your relationship isn't in a valid space at the present time. Understanding how to pursue laying out a relationship that is genuine and certifiable can appear to be troublesome. In any case, in the event that you and your accomplice will invest the energy and follow the means referenced here, you also can arrive. Simply begin dealing with your relationship together and your relationship will improve.

www.ingramcontent.com/pod-product-compliance
Lightning Source LLC
LaVergne TN
LVHW052110160826
845678LV00015B/3462

* 9 7 9 8 8 4 6 6 3 1 3 9 7 *